The Top Six THREATS to Civilization

NUCLEAR CONFRONTATION

Erin L. McCoy

Cavendish Square
New York

Published in 2019 by Cavendish Square Publishing, LLC
243 5th Avenue, Suite 136, New York, NY 10016

First Edition

Website: cavendishsq.com

Library of Congress Cataloging-in-Publication Data
Names: McCoy, Erin L., author.
Title: Nuclear confrontation / Erin L. McCoy.
Description: First edition. | New York : Cavendish Square, 2019. |
Series: The top six threats to civilization | Includes bibliographical references and index.
Identifiers: LCCN 2018026120 (print) | LCCN 2018030771 (ebook) |
ISBN 9781502641366 (ebook) | ISBN 9781502641359 (library bound) |
ISBN 9781502641342 (pbk.)
Subjects: LCSH: Nuclear warfare–Juvenile literature. |
Nuclear weapons–Juvenile literature. | Nuclear disarmament–Juvenile literature.
Classification: LCC U263 (ebook) | LCC U263 .M347 2019 (print) | DDC 355.02/17–dc23
LC record available at https://lccn.loc.gov/2018026120

Editorial Director: David McNamara
Copy Editor: Alex Tessman
Associate Art Director: Alan Sliwinski
Designer: Ginny Kemmerer
Production Coordinator: Karol Szymczuk
Photo Research: J8 Media

Portions of this book originally appeared in *Nuclear Annihilation* by Frank Spalding.

The photographs in this book are used by permission and through the courtesy of: Cover, Romolo Tavani/Shutterstock.com; background used throughout Tflex/Shutterstock.com; background used throughout iulias/Shutterstock.com; p. 4 Galerie Bilderwelt/Getty Images; p. 7 Flickr user Jim Linwood/https://www.flickr.com/photos/brighton/File: Nothe Fort nuclear shelter entrance.jpg/Wikimedia Commons/CCA 2.0 Generic; p. 8 Michael Dunning/Photographer's Choice/Getty Images; p. 11 Los Alamos National Laboratory/The LIFE Picture Collection/Getty Images; p. 13 Corbis/ Getty Images; p. 14 Cpl. Lynn P. Walker, Jr. (Marine Corps)/File: Nagasaki temple destroyed.jpg/Wikimedia Commons/Public Domain; p.16 Sovfoto/UIG/Getty Images; p. 18 Peter Menzel/Science Source; p. 19 AP Photo; (green background image) pp. 19, 33, 40, 48; pp. 21, 43 TASS/Getty Images; p. 22 WindVector/Shutterstock.com; p. 24 Mikhail Svetlov/Getty Images; p. 26 STR/AFP/Getty Images; p. 28 DIETER NAGL/AFP/Getty Images; p. 30 Ghaith Abdul-Ahad/Photonica World/Getty Images; p. 34 NARINDER NANU/AFP/Getty Images; p. 36 Korea Summit Press Pool/Getty Images; p. 37 JACK GUEZ/AFP/Getty Images; p. 39 DOE/ Science Source/Getty Images; p. 40 Herb Scharfman/The LIFE Images Collection/Getty Images; p. 45 Kyodo News/Getty Images; p. 50 DoD photo by Erin A. Kirk-Cuomo. (Released)/File: Indiana Sen. Richard Lugar, left, Secretary of Defense Leon E. Panetta, center, and former Georgia Sen. Sam Nunn 121203-D-BW835-497.jpg/Wikimedia Commons/Public Domain; p. 51LUDOVIC MARIN/AFP/Getty Images.

Printed in the United States of America

CONTENTS

INTRODUCTION: NUCLEAR WAR BREAKS OUT

The ground shivers, then begins to rise: an explosion, larger than you have ever seen or even imagined. A mountain of flame rises out of the earth, bubbling up in the shape of a mushroom, then expanding outward. A ripple of sound rushes toward you, demolishing trees, cars, and houses as it passes over them. No one will survive for miles around—the approaching wave of energy and destruction is too fast to outrun.

Elsewhere, farther from the blast site, frightened American families gather in front of their television sets. Emergency news broadcasts are playing on all the channels: another country has declared war on the United States, and has launched nuclear missiles that have struck some of the country's largest cities: New York, Los Angeles, Washington, DC. The US president has been killed in the attack, along with much of Congress, and the nation has been left without a clear leader.

Because of electrical disturbances throughout the country resulting from the bombs going off, the military is unable to effectively coordinate its national-defense efforts. Meanwhile, people attempt to flee the

Opposite: A nuclear test, comprised of a 914-kiloton thermonuclear air burst, is carried out near French Polynesia in the Pacific Ocean on May 22, 1970.

smoldering cities. The chaos and panicked crowds make it almost impossible for emergency services to help those injured in the explosions.

It seems that the United States has retaliated, and the attacking country, too, has suffered untold damage. Millions—perhaps hundreds of millions—have died. There's no way to know for sure. Meanwhile, every nation on the planet is on guard: who will be struck next? Whose side should they take in this escalating nuclear conflict, and what will happen when they do?

THE AFTERMATH

Of those who didn't die in the attacks, millions have suffered from horrific burns or are sick from nuclear radiation. Hospitals are overflowing with patients, many of whom will die before they can even receive medical attention. Radioactive dust and debris sent into the air from the nuclear explosions drifts on the wind, blanketing large parts of the country, even those that have not been attacked by bombs and missiles.

The United States becomes eerily quiet. Many of those who did not die from the explosions die of radiation poisoning in the next few hours, days, or weeks. Survivors are instructed to stay inside until the amount of radiation outside drops to a safe level. Riots break out as people fight over food and supplies.

The first survivors emerge from their shelters and see a bare, dead countryside. Dust and ash sent into the atmosphere from the bombs block the sunlight, causing an unnatural and unseasonable winter to descend over the land. Bands of survivors roam the landscape, sickened, diseased, and desperate for food and water that has not been contaminated by radiation, wondering if they will survive to see another year.

Many people built nuclear shelters during the Cold War. These were stocked with food and supplies, and were designed to protect occupants in the case of nuclear war.

IS THE THREAT REAL?

Could such a devastating nuclear war actually break out? Could civilization as we know it be destroyed by nuclear weapons? What events might lead to such a horrifying scenario? Many believe that such a war might result from escalating antagonisms between some of the world's most powerful countries: between the United States and Russia, North Korea and South Korea, India and Pakistan, or Israel and Iran.

As of mid-2018, nine nations were known to possess a total of about 14,500 nuclear weapons. The United States and Russia have the most weapons by far, at more than 6,500 each. These stockpiles were primarily built up during the Cold War, a period of nonviolent geopolitical tension between the two countries during the latter half of the twentieth century. North Korea, Israel, India, Pakistan, the United Kingdom, China, and France also possess nuclear weapons. Other nations have sought to develop them.

Many experts argue that nuclear war between countries is unlikely for a number of reasons, depending on each nation's situation. For North Korean leader Kim Jong Un, possessing nuclear weapons may be more advantageous than actually using them, political science professors Michael C. Horowitz and Elizabeth N. Saunders argued in

A US nuclear intercontinental ballistic missile is pictured in its silo in Arizona.

the *Washington Post* in January 2018. Kim "wants to stay in power, and nuclear weapons constitute invasion insurance. But a war probably would spell the end of the regime, giving North Korea little reason to start a war," they explained. Possessing nuclear weapons for the sake of discouraging other nations from using such weapons is a strategy known as nuclear deterrence. This approach, which has dominated international relations since the mid-twentieth century, is based on the belief that mutually assured destruction can lead to a kind of stability and even peace. As British prime minister Winston Churchill explained in 1955, "Safety will be the sturdy child of terror, and survival the twin brother of annihilation."

Many say that such a policy has averted World War III. Others insist that there is little evidence of this. Psychology professor David P. Barash argues in the *Guardian* newspaper that the United States' possession of nuclear weapons has not prevented wars with even nonnuclear weapon states or terrorist attacks such as those committed on September 11, 2001. He adds:

> Meanwhile, there are substantial risks associated with escalated conventional war, accidental or unauthorised use, irrational use (although it can be argued that any use of nuclear weapons would be irrational) or false alarms, which have happened with frightening regularity, and could lead to "retaliation" against an attack that hadn't happened.

Even assuming that nuclear deterrence works, if nuclear weapons fell into the hands of terrorists, they might not feel the same hesitancy. According to the Nuclear Threat Initiative, whose aim is to prevent catastrophic attacks, "increasingly well-organized and well-funded terrorist organizations—which now have easy access to the know-how needed to build a bomb—have declared their intent to seek the materials necessary for weapons of mass destruction."

Experts estimate the likelihood of human extinction as a result of nuclear weapons to be very low. However, even small nuclear conflicts can have global consequences. That's why it is so important to understand the many considerations that hang in the balance when it comes to nuclear weapons, denuclearization, and efforts toward global peace.

CHAPTER 1
THE NUCLEAR THREAT

In 1986, there were more than sixty thousand nuclear warheads on the planet. After that year, the number began to drop. With the end of the Cold War between the United States and the Soviet Union (now Russia), nuclear production facilities closed. Today, just a quarter of those weapons are still in existence.

Nuclear weapons remain the most powerful and destructive weapons in the world. If they were used in a nuclear war, life as we know it would change forever. Many people would be killed, and cities would be destroyed or made uninhabitable. Long-lasting environmental damage would be inflicted on the Earth's forests, rivers, and wildlife. A full-on nuclear war would have effects so devastating that they are virtually impossible to imagine.

To truly understand the threat of nuclear annihilation, we must understand how nuclear weapons came to be invented—and how they were first used.

Above: Dr. J. Robert Oppenheimer (*right*), a physicist, led the Manhattan Project, a US program that aimed to develop the most powerful weapon possible. He is pictured here with Leslie Groves, an army officer who directed the program.

Dr. J. Robert Oppenheimer (*white hat*) and other Manhattan Project officials inspect the detonation site after the first-ever atomic bomb test in 1945.

THE MANHATTAN PROJECT

Tens of millions of people died during the deadliest conflict in human history: World War II, fought between 1939 and 1945. Many were civilians. The war was fought between two different factions. On one side were the Axis powers, which included Nazi Germany, Fascist Italy, and Imperial Japan. On the other side were the Allied powers, including England, the Soviet Union, and the United States. The goal of the Axis powers was to dominate the world. The Allies fought to stop them.

In 1939, physicists Leó Szilárd and Albert Einstein wrote a letter to US president Franklin Delano Roosevelt. The letter warned Roosevelt that scientists had recently made a breakthrough by splitting the atom for the first time. They had discovered that when an atom was split, it released an incredible amount of energy. This could result in a process known as a nuclear chain reaction, which could create a very powerful explosion. Szilárd and Einstein thought that nuclear energy could be harnessed to create a superpowerful new weapon: a bomb capable of creating the largest explosion the world had ever seen.

At the time, the United States hadn't yet entered World War II. Many Americans believed that the war overseas was none of the United States' business. However, on December 7, 1941, Japanese planes attacked a US military base in Pearl Harbor, Hawaii. The United States could no longer remain neutral.

In 1942, President Roosevelt initiated a program to develop the most powerful weapon in history. The program, known as the Manhattan Project, was led by physicist J. Robert Oppenheimer. He established a number of secret laboratories where some of the most brilliant scientists in the world gathered to build a nuclear weapon before the Axis powers could build their own. The Manhattan Project was successful in achieving this goal, though it unleashed a terrible, destructive force on the world that continues to haunt us to this day.

HIROSHIMA AND NAGASAKI

At approximately 8:15 a.m. on August 6, 1945, the United States dropped a nuclear bomb on the Japanese city of Hiroshima. World War II was winding down, but Japan refused to surrender. The United States hoped to force it to do so with a show of overwhelming force.

The effects of the bomb were immediate and horrifying. The blast from the explosion leveled most of the city, instantly killing tens of thousands of people. Those nearest the spot where the bomb was dropped were immediately vaporized. People farther away suffered serious or deadly burns, and many were disfigured for the rest of their lives. Others received lethal doses of radiation. Dust and ash from the explosion rose into the atmosphere and then rained down on the city. Survivors described this fallout as "black rain."

On August 9, 1945, a second nuclear weapon was dropped on the Japanese city of Nagasaki. The Japanese government soon surrendered to the Allies. World War II was over. In Hiroshima, the death toll from the initial blast and its aftereffects eventually rose to approximately 200,000 people. In Nagasaki, an estimated 140,000 people were killed. Both cities were completely devastated.

The city of Nagasaki, Japan, sits in ruins on September 24, 1945, six weeks after the United States dropped an atomic bomb on the city with the aim of bringing a decisive end to World War II.

THE POWER OF THE BOMB

The bombs dropped on Hiroshima and Nagasaki remain the only nuclear weapons ever used in an act of war. The bomb dropped on Hiroshima had an estimated yield of 15 kilotons, the equivalent of 15,000 tons of TNT. Nevertheless, these bombs were relatively small by today's standards.

The center of a nuclear explosion can reach temperatures of 10 million degrees Fahrenheit (5,555,538 degrees Celsius), hotter than the surface of the sun. In fact, the first bomb ever tested, in the desert of New Mexico, actually fused the sand of the desert into glass. The intense heat vaporizes nearly everything within a quarter of a mile (0.4 kilometers) of ground zero. The explosion is so bright that those who look at it directly suffer eye damage, sometimes blindness. The shockwave from the blast can kill every human being up to 1 mile (1.6 km) away from the explosion site.

This horrifying destruction can be accomplished by a 15-kiloton bomb. However, the largest nuclear weapon ever tested, the Soviet-made bomb Czar Bomba, had an estimated yield of 100 megatons. This bomb was approximately 6,500 times more powerful than the bombs dropped on Hiroshima and Nagasaki.

The mechanical components of nuclear weapons may vary, but all contain either the element plutonium or certain types of the element uranium. When plutonium or uranium is used to create an explosion, the energy released raises the temperature around the element so much that it creates a massive blast wave. Nuclear explosions also emit electromagnetic fields, which can disrupt electrical systems and devices. Thermal radiation is released as well, causing a huge and destructive firestorm.

Czar Bomba was the most powerful nuclear weapon ever tested, thousands of times more powerful than the bombs dropped at Nagasaki and Hiroshima.

Uranium and plutonium are radioactive substances. As such, they can be harmful to plants and animals, as well as to human beings. Nuclear radiation lingers on after the explosion has ended, contaminating land and water. Radiation from many American and Soviet nuclear tests in the 1950s and 1960s can still be detected today. In the event of a nuclear war, radiation could remain in the environment and poison survivors. Radiation poisoning, also known as radiation sickness, is characterized by nausea, vomiting, diarrhea, and hair loss. If serious enough, it can result in seizures, coma, or even death. The long-term effects of radiation exposure can include cancer and sterility, which is the inability to have children.

Some scientists have speculated that a so-called nuclear winter could occur in the event of a massive nuclear war. Dust and ash from numerous nuclear explosions could block enough sunlight to lower the Earth's surface temperature and create a murky, perpetual winter-like environment. Others have speculated that atmospheric nuclear explosions (explosions detonated high above the planet's surface) could seriously deplete the planet's ozone layer. This would further expose survivors to illness—primarily sunburns, sun poisoning, and skin cancer.

If one nuclear weapon could destroy thriving cities like Hiroshima and Nagasaki, what could a hundred nuclear weapons do? Or a thousand? Could nuclear weapons kill every human being on Earth? This question became a serious concern in the period following World War II, when the United States and the Soviet Union, former allies, became the world's preeminent superpowers—and bitter rivals.

THE COLD WAR

The Union of Soviet Socialist Republics (USSR), or Soviet Union, was a Communist country that existed from 1922 to 1991. Extending from Europe across the full width of continental Asia, the USSR was comprised of present-day Russia, as well as fourteen surrounding countries. The United States and the USSR were huge countries with large populations, and they had conflicting political philosophies. After World War II, both the United States and the USSR tried to become the world's most important superpower. Although the two nations did not engage in direct conflict, they began amassing weapons for a possible future clash.

This arms race, known as the Cold War, was especially serious because the United States and the Soviet Union developed massive stockpiles of nuclear weapons. At its peak, the USSR had approximately forty-five thousand nuclear weapons, and the United States had approximately thirty-two thousand. For decades, the citizens of both nations lived in the very real fear that, one day, they might awaken to the sound of air-raid sirens alerting them that certain destruction was headed their way.

In 1991, the Soviet Union collapsed, breaking up into fifteen separate countries. The Cold War was finally over. However, the United States and the country now known again as Russia were left with thousands of nuclear weapons, all of them still very deadly.

A fire is started intentionally in order to obscure the sun and simulate a nuclear winter, in which sunlight would be blocked by excessive smoke, causing temperatures to drop, perhaps even on a global scale.

The Nuclear Dealings of A. Q. Khan

Abdul Qadeer Khan is believed to have secretly helped Iran develop its nuclear program.

Abdul Qadeer (A. Q.) Khan was born in India in 1936, but moved to Pakistan as a young man. Later, he traveled to Amsterdam in Europe to work at a research laboratory. While there, Khan stole classified documents from the lab. After his return to Pakistan, he was chosen to head his country's nuclear program. Pakistan set up a nuclear laboratory as early as 1976 and tested its first nuclear weapons in 1998.

Khan was not content with simply working to improve Pakistan's nuclear infrastructure. It is believed that, by the mid-1980s, he began exporting nuclear components. Khan secretly cooperated with Iran on its nuclear program, and he reportedly tried to sell Iraq a nuclear weapon. In February 2004, Khan made a public confession about his activities, adding that he had also helped Libya and North Korea develop their nuclear weapons technology. He was placed under house arrest but was released in 2009.

OTHER NUCLEAR MATERIALS

It is believed that some unaccounted-for nuclear weapons exist around the world, primarily in the former Soviet Union. Should such weapons fall into the hands of an aggressive nation or terrorist group, the consequences for the world could be very dire.

The process used to create nuclear power—an energy source—is not far removed from the process used to create nuclear weapons. Any nation with working nuclear power plants already has nearly everything it needs to manufacture a nuclear weapon. Nuclear power plants also contain materials that can be stolen and used to make nuclear weapons. Waste from nuclear power plants can be used to create dirty bombs. Terrorists might target nuclear facilities in an attempt to destroy them or steal nuclear materials that could be made into weapons. While every nuclear power plant in the United States has a security force, most would not be up to repelling a determined group of trained soldiers, armed and intent upon breaking in and stealing radioactive material.

So long as nuclear materials exist in the world, there is some danger that they may be used to wage war or wreak havoc and destruction. Countless governments, organizations, and experts are working to prevent this, but when it comes to nuclear confrontations, the worst-case scenarios can seem very frightening indeed.

CHAPTER 2
NUCLEAR CONFRONTATION SCENARIOS

Nuclear war on a global scale could lead to millions of deaths, raze entire cities, and severely damage the environment. Humans, animals, and plants would all be subject to severe health problems as a result of destruction at blast sites, radiation exposure, dust in the air, ozone layer depletion, and other effects. Nuclear winter could shroud the globe in darkness for years.

If nuclear war is so dangerous, why would anyone ever use a nuclear weapon? Even though it seems that no objective could be worth such devastation, consider how many people have been killed in the last one hundred years by conventional weapons. According to Robert McNamara, the US secretary of state under Presidents John F. Kennedy and Lyndon B. Johnson, an estimated 160 million people were killed in wars and other violent conflicts in the twentieth century. That's roughly equivalent to half the population of the United States. It's possible that even more people will be killed in violent conflicts in the twenty-first century without the help of nuclear weapons. If nuclear weapons are used, these numbers could be much, much higher. These are some of the worst-case scenarios that could result.

Above: A Bulava missile—a type of missile that takes off from a submarine—is launched during a Russian military drill on the Pacific coast of Russia in 2018.

NUCLEAR PROLIFERATION

The spread of nuclear material and weapons to other, previously nonnuclear weapon states is known as nuclear proliferation. Various factors inspire countries to acquire nuclear weapons. Some countries want to acquire nuclear weapons for defense and security purposes. For instance, when India acquired nuclear weapons, rival nation Pakistan felt threatened and began developing its own nuclear program. Nuclear stockpiles are also an international symbol of prestige and influence. Just nine countries are nuclear powers. Joining that group can be attractive for a country that wants to be taken seriously, to influence world events, or to have a bargaining chip in international negotiations.

While most countries carefully monitor their nuclear material and keep it very secure, there are some nations that are not as careful. Unfortunately, it is possible that these unsecured nuclear weapons could

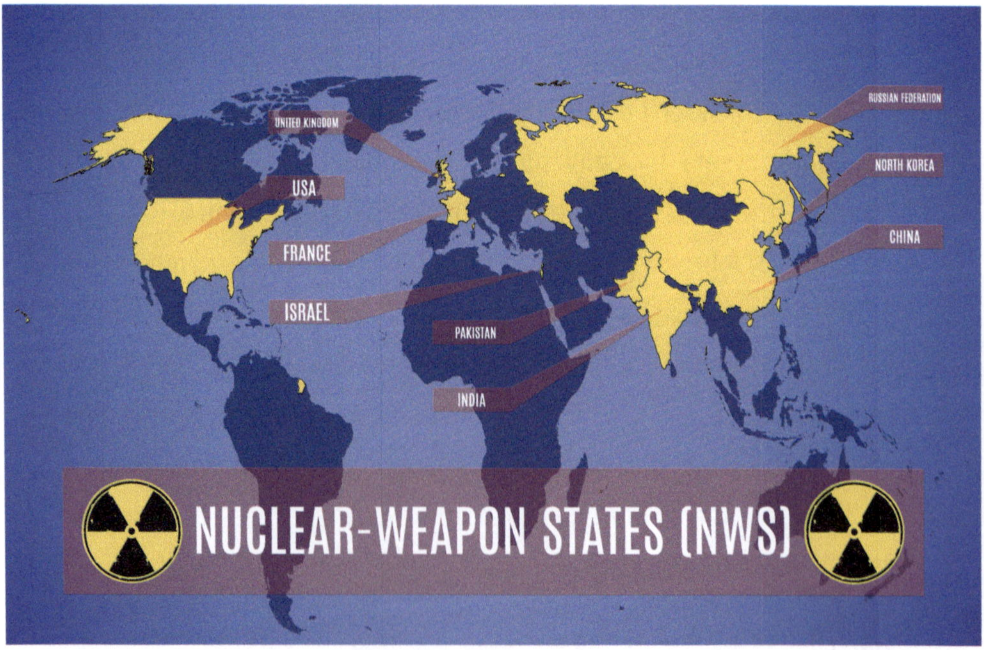

The nine countries known to possess nuclear weapons are shown in yellow.

fall into the hands of terrorists. It is one of the gravest threats to global security in the twenty-first century.

Each nation has its own reasons for building and maintaining a nuclear arsenal. Here are a few of those countries.

THE UNITED STATES

The United States is one of just two countries in the world to have nuclear weapons numbering in the thousands—approximately 6,550 in total, as of early 2018. It has also conducted more tests of such weapons than any other country, for a total of about 1,030 between 1945 and 1992.

Since the end of the Cold War, however, the United States, like Russia, has reduced the number of nuclear weapons in its arsenal. President Barack Obama envisioned a "world without nuclear weapons," and his administration's 2010 "Nuclear Posture Review" asserted that the United States "will not use or threaten to use nuclear weapons against non-nuclear weapons states," adding that the country's nuclear weapons were for self-defense only.

However, nuclear arsenals may be expanding again. A 2018 "Nuclear Posture Review" issued by the Donald Trump administration recommended adding two types of nuclear warheads to the US arsenal. It also suggested that the country might use nuclear weapons in response to nonnuclear attacks. Meanwhile, on March 1, 2018, President Vladimir Putin of Russia announced that his country was developing a new type of nuclear weapon that could be used on a missile with "basically an unlimited range." These events combined with the rising influence of China may constitute the beginning of a "New Cold War," according to Michael T. Klare, a professor of peace and world-security studies writing for the *Nation*. On the other hand, Michael E. O'Hanlon, a senior fellow for foreign policy at the Brookings Institution, a nonprofit public policy organization, believes the "Nuclear Posture Review" might make the world safer by sending a message that the United States is prepared to respond if Russia continues to develop weapons.

RUSSIA

Today, Russia has an estimated 6,800 nuclear weapons, the most in the world. It is the only country to have more than the United States.

The USSR had a large amount of nuclear material within its borders. This material still exists in Russia and the other countries that comprised the former Soviet Union. Some of this nuclear material is believed to be unsecured today. In a region that has undergone major political

During his March 1, 2018, state-of-the-union address, Russian president Vladimir Putin announced that Russia was working to develop a new kind of nuclear weapon.

and economic upheavals in the past twenty years, it is possible that corrupt government and military officials might be willing to sell nuclear materials for a profit. While the Russian government won't acknowledge that any nuclear weapons have gone missing, they have admitted that some nuclear material has been stolen.

PAKISTAN

Pakistan is another recognized nuclear power, with an estimated 130 to 140 nuclear weapons. It is also a nation long affected by political and cultural divisions in the region. It was once a part of its neighbor, India. In the decades since the two nations have been separated, there have been periodic clashes in border areas, and tensions remain high between the two countries. Pakistan is a predominantly Islamic nation, with a secular (nonreligious) government. However, there are political factions in Pakistan that would like the country to adopt a more conservative, religion-based government.

Pakistani scientist A. Q. Khan sold nuclear secrets to Iran, North Korea, and Libya. It is believed that Khan's network was made up of many influential people, maybe even members of the Pakistani government. Also, it is known that terrorists, including members of al-Qaeda, are hiding in Pakistan. These groups would almost certainly like to acquire enough nuclear materials to make dirty bombs.

NORTH KOREA

An extremely repressive and authoritarian dictatorship, North Korea became a nuclear weapons state in 2006. Led by absolute ruler Kim Jong Un, North Korea practices a severe form of communism in which its citizens live in extreme poverty and have no civil rights whatsoever.

Financially mismanaged, subjected to international sanctions, and isolated from the rest of the world, North Korea has virtually fallen apart under Kim Jong Un, as during the regime of his father, Kim Jong Il. Dependent upon humanitarian aid, North Korea has faced massive famines and malnourishment for years.

Both Kim Jong Il and Kim Jong Un have spent a great deal of North Korea's scant capital on its military, including a nuclear weapons program. North Korea manufactures long-range ballistic missiles, which can deliver a nuclear payload over a long distance. It has also withdrawn from the Nuclear Non-Proliferation Treaty (NPT), a major United Nations

North Korean leader Kim Jong Un (*fourth from left*) inspects an apparent weapon in a photograph released in September 2017. North Korea had reportedly developed a hydrogen bomb.

(UN) treaty designed to halt nuclear weapons development and monitor nuclear states. Considering how desperate North Korea is for money, and how hostile it is to the idea of global cooperation and international law, it is possible that it would be willing to sell nuclear materials or knowledge to terrorists intent on building a nuclear arsenal.

Today, it is estimated that North Korea has between ten and twenty nuclear weapons. However, in the first half of 2018, there was some renewed hope that North Korea might be willing to compromise on its nuclear arsenal, whose existence has provoked sanctions prohibiting international trade with the country. In February, North Korea marched alongside South Korea, usually considered a rival, in the Winter Olympics. In March, the United States and North Korea announced that its leaders would meet for the first time, and the next month, Kim Jong Un had an amicable meeting with Moon Jae In, the leader of South Korea. Kim Jong Un had indicated his willingness to denuclearize, potentially in exchange for foreign aid or lifted sanctions—though some have expressed doubt as to whether he was sincere.

The road to peaceful discussions has remained rocky. In May, North Korea insisted that preplanned military drills conducted by the United States and South Korea were a "provocation," and US president Donald Trump temporarily cancelled the planned meeting. The meeting, however, did take place on June 12, 2018, in Singapore. After the meeting, the two leaders issued a joint statement calling for the "complete denuclearization" of North Korea. However, many criticized the statement for not outlining a specific timeline for this process or specifying how North Korea might go about relinquishing its weapons. It remained unclear what the future might hold.

IRAN

Iran is a Middle Eastern nation that has, in the past, actively worked to acquire nuclear power and to develop a nuclear weapons program. Iran is known to fund Hamas, a fundamentalist Islamic organization based in the Palestinian territories. Hamas is dedicated to destroying Israel and replacing it with an Islamic nation. Hamas also has a history of using violent methods, including terrorism, to achieve this goal. If Iran is willing to support a terrorist organization financially, would it also be willing to supply such an organization with nuclear weapons?

In response to rumors that Iran was working toward developing nuclear weapons, the United States instituted sanctions in 2012 against any central banks of governments purchasing Iranian oil. The sanctions hurt Iran's economy. In 2015, the United Nations Security Council endorsed the Joint Comprehensive Plan of Action (JCPOA), in which Iran

European Union and Iranian members of the Joint Comprehensive Plan of Action (JCPOA), designed to reduce Iran's nuclear capabilities, meet in Austria in 2015.

committed to reducing the number of nuclear centrifuges it was using by two-thirds and disabling an important piece of its Arak nuclear reactor. In return, sanctions were lifted. However, when President Trump came into office in 2017, he argued that the JCPOA was the "worst deal in history," in part because it had an expiration date, and in May 2018 he withdrew from the pact. Leaders from France, Germany, and the United Kingdom had all personally lobbied Trump to stick to the deal.

CHINA

China has an estimated 270 nuclear weapons and conducted an estimated forty-five nuclear tests between 1964 and 1996. The United States' 2018 "Nuclear Posture Review" outlined a "tailored deterrence policy" regarding China's nuclear abilities. The goal was to prevent regional conflicts, which could escalate into nuclear conflicts. The report also said that China has "entirely new nuclear capabilities." In fact, there is some evidence that China is indeed secretly building its nuclear stockpiles.

DIRTY BOMBS

Not all nuclear weapons require advanced scientific knowledge to build. Nuclear material is very dangerous. Ordinarily, the byproducts created at nuclear power plants are carefully monitored and disposed of. This nuclear waste is, by itself, dangerous enough to kill people.

If terrorists were to get their hands on nuclear waste, they could use conventional explosives such as dynamite to create a dirty bomb that would disperse this radioactive waste. Used in a crowded city like New York, a dirty bomb could harm or kill many thousands of people within a small area. Moreover, it could contaminate the surrounding

Terrorist groups around the world already use bombs as one of their preferred weapons, as was the case when this car bomb was detonated near a school in Baghdad, Iraq, in 2005.

area where it was used, resulting in the illness or death of many others not affected by the initial explosion.

Dirty bombs could provide terrorists with a crude, but still very deadly, way to wreak havoc and spread fear. The material used to build dirty bombs could be stolen from nuclear facilities anywhere in the world, including the United States.

THE TERRORIST THREAT

The increase in terrorist activity around the world has given rise to fears of nuclear terrorism. Unlike nation-states, terrorist groups are not generally worried about damaging their public image or their relationships with nations they consider enemies. They also can't be held to international treaties. Terrorist groups are difficult, if not impossible, to negotiate with, and they work independently from the countries in which they are based. Some may be made up of individual cells that have no knowledge of the activities of other cells within the group. This further complicates any attempt to target, deal with, or negotiate with a terrorist organization, especially one that may have no central authority.

Terrorist groups are generally comprised of people who hold extreme beliefs. Neither the group nor its beliefs or actions tend to gain much public support. This is why terrorists are willing to resort to violence against innocent civilians: they aren't trying to gain popularity like most leaders and politicians are. If terrorists are willing to lose everything—even their lives—for their beliefs, they won't be deterred in their murderous actions by public outcry or persuaded to lay down their arms by attempts at diplomacy.

Certainly, the concern that terrorists could make a dirty bomb is a pressing one. However, if terrorists were able to acquire or fashion a small-yield nuclear weapon—for instance, a 10-kiloton bomb, smaller than the bomb dropped on Hiroshima but much more powerful than a crude dirty bomb—the results would be much more frightening. If such a bomb were detonated in midtown Manhattan, it would destroy every building within a third of a mile (0.5 km) of the explosion. Buildings nearly a mile (1.6 km) from this circle of destruction would also be damaged. If this explosion occurred during an average workday, hundreds of thousands of people would be killed. Fires caused by the blast could affect structures within a mile and a half (2.4 km) of the epicenter of the explosion.

Assuming that the terrorist group that detonated the bomb could be identified, the United States—and, most likely, a coalition of its allies—might launch an offensive to hunt down and destroy the attackers. If these terrorists were hiding in a nuclear nation, such as Pakistan, the situation might become even more complicated. If the United States were to respond with nuclear force, it could be seen as a direct act of aggression against the country in which the terrorists were hiding. The use of nuclear weapons in this scenario would mark the first time since World War II that such weapons were used in an act of war. Such a nuclear attack could lead to a chain reaction of nuclear responses that could result in a large-scale, multiparty nuclear war with hundreds of devastated targets.

NUCLEAR WAR SCENARIOS

The threat of nuclear war has hung over the world for more than sixty years. The horror of the bombings of Hiroshima and Nagasaki is almost too extreme for the human mind to comprehend. Thousands of such bombings within just a few days or even hours of each other are unthinkable—but definitely possible. How could a full-on conventional war between two nuclear-capable nations lead to such an event?

PAKISTAN AND INDIA

Neighboring rivals India and Pakistan have managed to acquire an estimated 250 nuclear weapons or more between them. India tested its first nuclear weapon in 1974, and Pakistan conducted its first nuclear

False Alarm

In 1995, Russian radar detected a Norwegian rocket. This rocket was not a weapon. It had actually been launched for research purposes. However, there was no way to tell that from the radar. In fact, to the Russians, the rocket looked like a US-launched missile. A countdown to a possible nuclear strike was initiated. Russian president Boris Yeltsin was prepared to launch the brunt of Russia's considerable nuclear might at the United States. However, after almost ten minutes passed, the Russians realized their mistake and stood down.

This incident highlighted the weakness of our nuclear defenses. While we ponder global politics and conflict, we must also consider that simple error—rather than aggression and malice—might bring about nuclear annihilation. The chance that a nuclear weapon might be launched accidentally, precipitating a nuclear war, is very real.

test in 1998. Pakistan and India broke apart in 1947, and the two nations have had tense relations ever since. The dominant religion in Pakistan is Islam; in India, it is Hinduism. The two nations have clashed over territory before, and some worry that future clashes could escalate into nuclear war.

Besides the extensive destruction that a nuclear war would cause to both nations, there is a danger that a nuclear conflict between India and Pakistan could spread to other countries. Islamic extremists outside the region might begin targeting Indians. Or terrorists might use the war to recruit supporters in Pakistan and elsewhere to spread chaos and conflict more widely.

A daily ceremony takes place at the India-Pakistan border, carried out by the Pakistani Rangers (*in black uniforms*) and the Indian Border Security Force (*in brown uniforms*). Tensions between these two nuclear powers are often elevated for territorial, political, and religious reasons.

NORTH KOREA AND SOUTH KOREA

North Korea is believed to have a very small nuclear arsenal of ten to twenty weapons, developed in part with the assistance of A. Q. Khan. Although a very poor nation, North Korea heavily invests its scant financial resources in its military, which comprises approximately one million soldiers.

The formerly united nation of Korea was split into two countries after World War II. South Korea became allied with the United States, and communist North Korea became allied with the Soviet Union. In 1950, North Korean troops invaded South Korea. Within three years, a cease-fire was declared, but the war between the two states has never officially ended.

North Korea has few allies and has proved remarkably resilient against diplomatic efforts to disarm its nuclear program and draw it back within the international community. South Korea maintains strong alliances with the United States and Japan, and both countries would certainly stage a military intervention if North Korea attacked South Korea. The sheer size of North Korea's army would guarantee a long and difficult war.

ISRAEL AND IRAN

Israel is the United States' strongest ally in the Middle East. The tiny nation has gone to war with its neighbors many times over the years. With roughly eighty weapons, by some estimates, it is the only nuclear weapons state in the region. Still, it neither confirms nor denies having such weapons.

In the last few decades, another Middle Eastern country, Iran, has developed a rivalry with Israel. Former Iranian president Mahmoud

South Korean president Moon Jae In (*right*) and North Korean leader Kim Jong Un clasp hands after signing the Panmunjom Declaration for Peace, Prosperity, and Unification of the Korean Peninsula on April 27, 2018.

Ahmadinejad even called for the "annihilation" of Israel. Iran has attempted to develop nuclear power, but any country with a functioning nuclear power plant could also make a nuclear weapon. In fact, on March 1, 2008, Admiral Mike Mullin, of the Joint Chiefs of Staff, stated on CNN's "State of the Union" that the United States believed Iran had enough uranium to make a nuclear weapon. Such observations led to the sanctions that in turn led to the JCPOA.

Israel is a very small country. In fact, it is approximately the size of New Jersey. Just a few nuclear weapons could wipe out all of Israel's major cities. Since Israel is a nuclear weapons state, a first strike by Iran would almost certainly prompt an Israeli nuclear counterstrike.

A nuclear war between Iran and Israel could drag other nations into a larger war. An Iranian nuclear strike on Israel could invite US or UN intervention. If Israel counterattacked Iran with a nuclear weapon, it is very likely that Iran's allies would rally to support it. Suddenly, a far larger war between the West and the East could erupt. The Middle East, long a powder keg of regional and global tension and conflict, could finally explode. The devastating results would affect nearly every nation in the world, even those far from the region and politically neutral.

During a 2018 joint military exercise, a US Patriot missile defense system (*right*) and an Israeli Iron Dome anti-rocket system (*left*) are visible.

RUSSIA AND THE UNITED STATES

For decades, the United States and the Soviet Union were adversaries. Emerging as the world's two great superpowers following World War II, both nations began stockpiling nuclear weapons. For decades during the Cold War, these countries teetered on the brink of nuclear conflict.

Today, following the breakup of the Soviet Union, Russia remains a massive political power. Struggling with political and economic changes, Russia is no longer a communist country. However, many have argued that it is also not a true democracy. As the largest nation in the world, Russia is still very powerful, and it is actively trying to expand its strength and influence.

While the United States and Russia are currently not officially considered adversaries, the two nations disagree on many political issues. Controversy over Russian meddling in the 2016 US presidential election as well as growing nuclear arsenals on both sides have heightened these tensions. Should current antagonisms escalate into full-scale nuclear war, the conflict could be devastating. Between them, the two countries possess an estimated 92 percent of all the world's nuclear weapons, just a fraction of which could destroy humanity as we know it.

CHAPTER 3
ASSESSING THE THREAT

Given how much war, violence, and terrorism the world has faced—and still faces—on a daily basis, worst-case scenarios around nuclear annihilation may seem frighteningly possible. However, global leaders and organizations are working hard to ensure that no nuclear weapon is ever deployed again.

The chances of nuclear terrorism happening are relatively low. Thankfully, it isn't easy for terrorists to get their hands on nuclear weapons. What's more, building a nuclear weapon requires a great deal of specialized knowledge and equipment, so it's very unlikely that any terrorist group would have the resources or know-how to build such a bomb.

There are many other obstacles to worst-case nuclear annihilation scenarios, including technical obstacles, reduced nuclear stockpiles, international pacts and oversight, global sanctions, and shifting political attitudes toward both nuclear weapons and membership within the international community.

Above: Uranium-235 is the radioactive isotope of uranium use to fuel nuclear reactors—and nuclear weapons. This "button" weighs about 9.9 pounds (4.5 kilograms) and is valued at roughly $200,000.

Atoms for Peace

President Dwight D. Eisenhower is pictured shortly before delivering his "Atoms for Peace" speech on December 8, 1953.

In 1953, US president Dwight D. Eisenhower delivered his "Atoms for Peace" speech to the UN General Assembly. In this talk, he put forth a bold vision of a future in which atomic power would be used for peaceful purposes and the arms race would come to an end:

> The United States would seek more than the mere reduction or elimination of atomic materials for military purposes. It is not enough to take this weapon out of the hands of the soldiers. It must be put into the hands of those who will know how to strip its military casing and adapt it to the arts of peace. The United States knows that if the fearful trend of atomic military buildup can be reversed, this greatest of destructive forces can be developed into a great boon, for the benefit of all mankind.

TECHNICAL OBSTACLES

More than 99 percent of the world's nuclear material is accounted for and protected by heavy security. Plutonium is very rare and would be extraordinarily expensive to purchase. Weapons-grade uranium is similarly rare and expensive. Standard uranium can be "enriched," or made into the kind of uranium that can be used to create a nuclear weapon. But again, this process requires specialized knowledge and precision equipment. Enriching uranium is not only beyond the capabilities of a terrorist group, but it is beyond the capabilities of most countries. Should a terrorist group purchase or steal highly enriched uranium or plutonium, it would be faced with the difficulty of how to actually work with it. Both of these substances are radioactive and very dangerous, even deadly.

Unsecured nuclear weapons, such as those believed to be in the former Soviet Union, also present a set of problems for a terrorist group or rogue nation. Like many other complicated pieces of machinery, nuclear weapons require regular maintenance, or they will cease to function properly. It is possible that, should a terrorist group purchase a stolen nuclear weapon on the black market, it might not still be in working order. Also, most nuclear weapons come equipped with complex safeguards that prevent unauthorized individuals from detonating them.

REDUCED NUCLEAR STOCKPILES

The number of nuclear weapons in existence reached its apex during the Cold War. Since then, the United States and Russia have greatly reduced their nuclear stockpiles. Some nations have agreed to do away with their nuclear programs altogether. As a result, in the event of nuclear war, there would simply be fewer nuclear weapons available.

Out of all the countries that have the technological and financial capacity to build or acquire nuclear weapons, very few have actually done so. Most nuclear-capable nations have found that the costs of having such weapons far outweigh the benefits.

INTERNATIONAL PACTS AND OVERSIGHT

The United Nations' International Atomic Energy Agency (IAEA) carefully monitors all nuclear materials. Established in 1957, the IAEA is an organization dedicated to promoting peaceful uses for nuclear energy and preventing the proliferation, or spread, of nuclear weapons worldwide. To this end, the agency and its director, Mohamed ElBaradei, were recognized by the Nobel Institute in 2005, when they were awarded a Nobel Peace Prize.

One of the most important functions the IAEA performs is monitoring nuclear material. The Nuclear Non-Proliferation Treaty (NPT) was designed by the IAEA to stop the spread of nuclear weapons. It was put into effect in 1970. Countries that sign the treaty agree to submit to intensive IAEA inspections regarding their nuclear activities. Safe, peaceful nuclear power and technology are generally more useful to nations than nuclear weapons are. The IAEA helps countries improve nuclear safety and security in order to prevent nuclear materials from falling into the hands of terrorists. The IAEA also works to stop the illegal procurement and sale of nuclear materials.

Currently, about 160 nations have signed the NPT and are working alongside the IAEA to ensure that they have safe and peaceful nuclear futures. Nations that refuse to cooperate with the IAEA may face sanctions and other punishments from the international community.

GLOBAL SANCTIONS

For new and aspiring nuclear weapons states, a number of outside factors make it unlikely that they will ever develop or use these weapons because doing so would be against their own best interests. International sanctions—penalties that restrict trade in commercial, medical, military, and even humanitarian goods to the rogue nation—are the primary tool used to deter countries from developing, testing, or using nuclear weapons. Such sanctions brought Iran to the negotiating table in talks that eventually led to a deal with the United States and other countries to cut Iran's nuclear development capacity.

Because North Korea manufactures long-range ballistic missiles, its nuclear developments have left many nations around the world uneasy. Economic sanctions against North Korea have proven detrimental—even

The Nuclear Non-Proliferation Treaty is signed by representatives of the United States (*left, at table*), the USSR (*center*), and Great Britain (*right*) on June 12, 1968, at a session of the United Nations General Assembly.

catastrophic—to the isolated, impoverished nation. Some argue that these sanctions were a primary motivator for Kim Jong Un in proposing denuclearization talks in early 2018.

SHIFTING POLITICAL ATTITUDES

While the threat of nuclear war is real, the world has changed considerably since the days when Americans were terrified of the possibility of the Cold War escalating into a global nuclear apocalypse. Nuclear weapons stockpiles have been decreasing for more than twenty years. Most nuclear countries are members of the United Nations and voluntarily submit to international supervision of their stockpiles. Those that don't are locked into a number of international alliances that they would be reluctant to damage. Strict nonproliferation protocols have ensured that the world has relatively few nuclear states.

For most nations, there are few advantages to developing nuclear weapons—in fact, many have given up on past intentions to do so. The world has thousands fewer nuclear weapons than it did thirty years ago, and many believe that the delicate balance that the international community has currently achieved can in fact lead to peace. What's more, for all the violent conflicts that the world has witnessed, global leaders have demonstrated again and again that they are not willing to deploy nuclear weapons. Not one has been deployed outside of testing sites since World War II.

CHAPTER 4

PREVENTING NUCLEAR CONFRONTATION

A great deal is being done to ensure that nuclear weapons are never used in violent conflict again. Many are even advocating for complete denuclearization around the globe, though that goal would be harder to attain.

The development and proliferation of nuclear weapons has been carefully monitored since the dawn of the Atomic Age. If this hadn't been the case, we could very well be living in a world with many more nuclear states than exist today. Reducing the chance of a full-out nuclear war revolves around a few simple principles.

NONPROLIFERATION

When nations have acquired nuclear weapons for national security purposes, they have often done so in response to a rival nation that has nuclear weapons. Having nuclear weapons transforms the relationship between countries and inevitably sparks further proliferation, increasing the chance of a nuclear conflict. This process must be stopped if we are to avoid nuclear annihilation. In fact, most experts agree that the

Above: Security guards stand at the entrance to a nuclear power plant in Oi, Japan, on July 2, 2012.

single best way to lessen the chance of nuclear war is to make sure that new countries don't get nuclear weapons.

In the Nuclear Non-Proliferation Treaty (NPT) signed in 1968, the United Kingdom, the Soviet Union, the United States, and many other nations agreed not to help other nations develop nuclear weapons. The treaty is still in effect. Many have argued that it is intrinsically unfair, since it permits just a few nuclear states to retain their weapons but prohibits the rest of the world from acquiring such arms.

DISARMAMENT

Stopping proliferation is one important step to achieving a world that is free of nuclear weapons. Actually reversing proliferation takes the world one step closer to a nuclear-free future. Some countries have voluntarily given up their nuclear weapons.

Activists wave signs in New York City on August 14, 2017, to protest sanctions and potential military action against North Korea.

For instance, throughout much of the second half of the twentieth century, South Africa was a deeply unpopular country because of its racist government policy known as apartheid. (This policy was formally ended in 1994.) Having begun to develop nuclear power under the Atoms for Peace program in 1957, South Africa eventually began to develop nuclear weapons. Ultimately, the nation decided that it would be to its benefit to cooperate with the IAEA. In 1991, it officially joined the NPT as a nonnuclear weapons state. South Africa believed that it would be more secure without nuclear weapons, so it disarmed its missiles.

AGGRESSIVE OVERSIGHT

The IAEA's role in preventing nuclear conflicts can hardly be overstated. Fewer countries have nuclear weapons in the twenty-first century than at any point from the 1960s through the 1980s. In addition, the number of nuclear weapons worldwide has been more than halved since 1986. Still, four nuclear countries—India, Pakistan, Israel, and North Korea—haven't signed the NPT.

Nevertheless, an overwhelming majority of world governments have signed the NPT, a fact that is not to be dismissed lightly. The public's perception of nuclear weapons has changed greatly since the Cold War. More people and governments see them as a source of danger instead of security. Most wish to see their elimination, rather than their increase and proliferation.

If North Korea agrees to completely renounce nuclear weapons and fully cooperate with the IAEA, it is very possible that a long-lasting era of nonproliferation can be brought about. The incentives offered to these countries by the UN to encourage them to end their programs

Giving Up Their Arsenals

After the breakup of the Soviet Union, three newly independent countries—Belarus, Kazakhstan, and Ukraine—found that they had nuclear weapons left over from the USSR. Between them, they had approximately four thousand nuclear weapons. Like South Africa, they also decided that they would be better off without nuclear stockpiles, so they got rid of them. Other nations that have ended their nuclear weapons programs include Libya, Brazil, and Argentina.

While in many cases, their lack of nuclear weapons has not compromised these nations' security, Joe Petrucelli, a senior analyst at Systems Planning and Analysis, Inc., argues that denuclearized states such as Libya are more likely to be involved in conflicts—often with nuclear powers. Denuclearization without first "resolving the underlying security threat" in a region, then, is not advisable, according to Petrucelli. He recommends that the United States must "offer more concrete security guarantees" if it truly wishes to achieve widespread denuclearization.

are considerable, as are the negative consequences if they continue to pursue these dangerous weapons.

The Comprehensive Nuclear-Test-Ban Treaty, instituted in 1996, places a global ban on nuclear weapons testing. The goal is to prevent the further development of weapons capabilities. Since newly developed weapons cannot be tested, those nations that have created them may feel less confident in using them, the US Department of State explains.

UNACCOUNTED-FOR NUCLEAR MATERIAL

Securing loose nuclear materials is one of the most significant actions that can be taken to reduce the likelihood of nuclear terrorism. Efforts to tackle this issue have included the Nunn-Lugar Soviet Nuclear Threat Reduction Act of 1991, which allocated funding for securing nuclear materials in former Soviet states.

Further action can be taken. Holding the United States and the world up to stricter nuclear security standards would be a crucial step toward preventing nuclear terrorism. Nuclear materials should be heavily guarded to prevent their theft.

INTERNATIONAL COOPERATION

The world we live in today is more interconnected than the world of sixty years ago. Globalization is transforming business and culture. New technologies allow people thousands of miles apart to communicate easily and effectively. News, music, film, television, fashion, and popular culture are instantly disseminated all over the world. The world is more open than it used to be, a process that will inevitably continue and have ramifications for political cooperation.

Then-Senator Richard Lugar (*left*), then-Secretary of Defense Leon Panetta (*center*), and former senator Sam Nunn are recognized in a 2012 ceremony for their work toward denuclearization following the fall of the Soviet Union.

Through international cooperation, we can ensure that warfare doesn't go nuclear. We can be aware of the nuclear capabilities of every country. We can encourage each nation to keep track of its nuclear arsenals and ensure that, should standing nuclear treaties be violated, those responsible will be brought to justice. Preventing the use of nuclear weapons is every nation's responsibility.

In addition, individual countries can be encouraged to devote time and resources to rooting out terrorist organizations within their borders. Terrorist cells usually have to depend on a larger group or collective for funding. Even the most secretive terrorist networks can be identified, located, and disrupted.

It is also important for every nation to play by the rules set down by the NPT. A lot of international attention has been focused on the four nations that have not signed this treaty—Israel, North Korea, India, and Pakistan. However, it is also important that those countries that have signed the treaty do not violate it. The NPT can only work if it is respected. So far, it has done much to prevent nuclear proliferation.

Successful international cooperation hinges on every country playing by the same set of rules. One of the biggest incentives for militarily weak nations to sign the NPT is that nations with powerful militaries and, in some cases, nuclear weapons or the potential to make them, have signed it as well. If international treaties such as the NPT aren't respected by its signatories, they can break down. This is why open, honest cooperation and fair play are necessary if we ever hope to rid ourselves of these dangerous weapons.

Anti-nuclear protestors gather in Aachen, Germany, on May 10, 2018. Their signs call for an end to Tihange and Doel, two nuclear-energy production sites in Belgium.

HOW YOU CAN HELP

In the United States, we are lucky to have our democratic freedoms, civil liberties, and civil rights. The right to free speech, the right to free assembly, and the right to vote gives individual citizens great power. However, with this power comes responsibility. Ultimately, you are responsible for helping determine the future of the world. If you want to live in a world without the threat of nuclear war, you have the power to work to make that happen.

It is never too early to learn more and think about ways to get involved. Joining the student government; volunteering at nonprofit organizations devoted to peace and nonproliferation; and lobbying local, state, and federal officials about nuclear issues are just some of the ways that you can get involved in the political process and add your voice to the debate.

Many colleges offer classes in political science, human rights, and international relations. You can study these and related subjects, and even launch a career in which you fight on the front lines to create a world that is finally free of the specter of nuclear annihilation. It is never too soon to get involved in shaping the world that you would like to live in and hand over to your children.

Nuclear nonproliferation, disarmament, and—perhaps one day—a world without nuclear weapons all demand international cooperation and a global commitment to peace. While these goals can seem impossible to reach, such solutions must be actively and carefully pursued in order to prevent future nuclear confrontation.

GLOSSARY

air-raid siren A siren that alerts the civilian population to an incoming assault by air.

amass To gather, collect, hoard, or stockpile.

annihilation Complete and utter destruction.

ballistic missile A missile fitted with a warhead that is capable of delivering its payload over a great distance.

contaminate To poison.

conventional explosives Nonnuclear explosives.

devastated Having suffered terrible destruction.

disarmament The withdrawal or reduction of military forces or weapons.

disrupt To break up or interrupt.

fallout The radioactive dust and other debris spread into the atmosphere after a nuclear explosion. Fallout often enters the atmosphere and then returns to Earth.

havoc Complete chaos.

humanitarian aid Assistance, such as food or medicine, provided to a needy country for humanitarian, or life-saving and life-sustaining, purposes.

nausea A feeling of sickness.

negotiate To bargain with.

nuclear deterrence Possessing nuclear weapons for the sake of discouraging other nations from using such weapons.

nuclear nonproliferation The prevention of the spread of nuclear weapons and related technologies to nations that are not yet nuclear weapon states.

perpetual Unending, or continuing for an indefinite amount of time.

sanction An economic punishment, such as fines or trade restrictions, imposed by one country or a group of countries on another.

shockwave A forceful disturbance created by a blast.

sterility The state of being unable to reproduce.

vaporize To change into a gas.

FURTHER INFORMATION

BOOKS

Brode, Harold L., and Larry MacDonald. *Nuclear Weapons in the Cold War*. Pacific Palisades, CA: Montgomery Publishing, 2014.

Ellsberg, Daniel. *The Doomsday Machine: Confessions of a Nuclear War Planner*. New York: Bloomsbury USA, 2017.

Larsen, Jeffrey A., and Kerry M. Kartchner. *On Limited Nuclear War in the 21st Century*. Stanford, CA: Stanford University Press, 2014.

Roberts, Brad. *The Case for U.S. Nuclear Weapons in the 21st Century*. Stanford, CA: Stanford University Press, 2016.

WEBSITES

Arms Control Association

https://www.armscontrol.org
The nonpartisan Arms Control Association offers a wealth of research and resources on nuclear treaties and weapons policy, in addition to country-specific weapons data.

Beyond Nuclear

http://www.beyondnuclear.org
This site advocates for the end of both nuclear weapons and nuclear power, offering information on renewable-energy alternatives and fact sheets on the health impacts of nuclear reactors.

United Nations Office for Disarmament Affairs

https://www.un.org/disarmament/wmd/nuclear
UNODA offers a number of publications, research tools, and databases about nuclear weapons and disarmament around the world.

VIDEOS

Animation Shows the Deadly Evolution of Nuclear Weapons

https://www.youtube.com/watch?v=xLRSmzGRLUk
A video from *Tech Insider* shows the size and blast radius of the bombs dropped on Hiroshima and Nagasaki in comparison with more modern nuclear weapons.

Nuclear Weapons: A Time-Lapse History

https://www.youtube.com/watch?v=gJe7fY-yowk
View a four-minute history of nuclear weapons development, including a map of where nuclear testing has occurred and at what frequency over time.

What Does Nuclear Fallout Do to Your Body?

https://www.youtube.com/watch?v=fYJ-FiRWY0c
Learn about the widespread health impacts that result when a nuclear bomb explodes.

ORGANIZATIONS

Canadians for a Nuclear Weapons Convention

43 Aylmer #358
Ottawa, K1S 5R4
http://nuclearweaponsconvention.ca
This organization seeks the establishment of a treaty on the elimination and prohibition of nuclear weapons.

Carnegie Endowment for International Peace

1779 Massachusetts Avenue NW
Washington, DC 20036-2103
(202) 483-7600
http://www.carnegieendowment.org
This nonprofit organization is dedicated to fostering peace by promoting international cooperation.

Center for Arms Control and Non-Proliferation
820 1st Street NE, Suite LL-180
Washington, DC 20002
(202) 546-0795
http://www.armscontrolcenter.org
This nonprofit, nonpartisan organization works to increase global security.

International Atomic Energy Agency
Vienna International Centre, PO Box 100
A-1400 Vienna, Austria
+43 (1) 2600-0
http://www.iaea.org
The IAEA monitors nuclear materials around the world in th interest of promoting peaceful uses for nuclear energy.

International Campaign to Abolish Nuclear Weapons
150 Route de Ferney, 1211
Genève 2, Switzerland
+41 22 788 20 63
http://www.icanw.org
ICAN is a group of nongovernmental organizations across one hundred nations dedicated to developing a nuclear-weapons-ban treaty.

Nuclear Threat Initiative
1776 Eye Street, NW, Suite 600
Washington, DC 20006
(202) 296-4810
http://www.nti.org
The Nuclear Threat Initiative is dedicated to reducing the threat of weapons of mass destruction by strengthening global security.

BIBLIOGRAPHY

"About." Nuclear Threat Initiative. Accessed May 24, 2018. http://www.nti.org/about.

"Acute Radiation Syndrome." Centers for Disease Control and Prevention. Retrieved February 2009. http://www.bt.cdc.gov/radiation/ars.asp.

"A. Q. Khan Nuclear Chronology." Carnegie Endowment for International Peace, September 7, 2005. http://www.carnegieendowment.org/static/npp/Khan_Chronology.pdf.

Baidi, Mubashir, and Laura King. "A. Q. Khan, Pakistani Nuclear Scientist, Freed by Pakistan Court." *Los Angeles Times*, February 6, 2009. http://www.latimes.com/news/nationworld/world/la-fg-pakistan-khan7-2009feb07,0,4151948.story.

Baum, Seth D. "Winter-Safe Deterrence: The Risk of Nuclear Winter and Its Challenge to Deterrence." *Contemporary Security Policy* 36, no. 1 (April 2015): 123–148. http://sethbaum.com/ac/2015_Deterrence.html.

Cirincione, Joseph. *Bomb Scare: The History and Future of Nuclear Weapons*. New York: Columbia University Press, 2007.

"Comprehensive Nuclear Test-Ban Treaty (CTBT)." US Department of State. Accessed May 24, 2018. https://www.state.gov/t/avc/c42328.htm.

Gertz, Bill. "US Tailors Forces to Deter Growing Chinese Nuclear Threat." *Asia Times*, March 5, 2018. http://www.atimes.com/article/us-tailors-forces-deter-growing-chinese-nuclear-threat.

Green, David B. "From Friends to Foes: How Israel and Iran Turned into Arch-enemies." *Haaretz*, May 8, 2018. https://www.haaretz.com/middle-east-news/iran/MAGAZINE-how-israel-and-iran-went-from-allies-to-enemies-1.6049884.

Hodgson, Martin. "North Korea Has Plutonium Ready for Up to Five Nuclear Bombs, Reports Claim." *Guardian* (UK), January 17, 2009. http://www.guardian.co.uk/world/2009/jan/17/northkorea-south-korea-nuclearweapons.

Horowitz, Michael C., and Elizabeth N. Saunders. "Why Nuclear War with North Korea Is Less Likely Than You Think." *Washington Post*, May 24, 2018. https://www.washingtonpost.com/news/monkey-cage/wp/2018/01/03/why-nuclear-war-with-north-korea-is-less-likely-than-you-think/?utm_term=.35a75729be0f.

"IAEA Primer: Maximizing the Contribution of Nuclear Technology to Society While Verifying Its Peaceful Use." International Atomic Energy Agency. Retrieved February 2009. http://www.iaea.org/Publications/Factsheets/English/iaea-primer.pdf.

Jenkins, Brian Michael. *Will Terrorists Go Nuclear*? Amherst, NY: Prometheus Books, 2008.

Klare, Michael T. "The New Cold War Is Here—and Now 3 Major Powers Are Involved." *Nation*, March 8, 2018. https://www.thenation.com/article/the-new-cold-war-is-here-and-now-three-major-powers-are-involved.

Kristensen, Hans M., and Robert S. Norris. "Nuclear Notebook: Nuclear Arsenals of the World." *Bulletin of the Atomic Scientists*, 2018. https://thebulletin.org/nuclear-notebook-multimedia.

Landler, Mark. "The Trump-Kim Summit Was Unprecedented, but the Statement Was Vague." *New York Times*, June 12, 2018. https://www.nytimes.com/2018/06/12/world/asia/north-korea-summit.html.

Leventhal, Paul L., Sharon Tanzer, and Steven Dolley, eds. *Nuclear Power and the Spread of Nuclear Weapons*. Dulles, VA: Brassey's, Inc., 2002.

Macias, Amanda. “There Are About 14,500 Nuclear Weapons in the World. Here Are the Countries That Have Them.” CNBC, March 16, 2018. https://www.cnbc.com/2018/03/16/list-of-countries-with-nuclear-weapons.html.

May, Andrew. “After the Cold War Where Did the Nuclear Weapons That the Soviet Union Possessed Go?” Classroom. Accessed May 24, 2018. https://classroom.synonym.com/after-cold-war-did-nuclear-weapons-soviet-union-possessed-go-21842.html.

Mo, Richard. “Author Sees Greater War Casualties.” *Daily Pennsylvanian*, June 14, 2001. http://media.www.dailypennsylvanian.com/media/storage/paper882/news/2001/06/14/News/Author.Sees.Greater.War.Casualties-2160801.shtml.

O’Hanlon, Michael E. “Trump’s Nuclear Plan Mostly Makes Sense.” Brookings Institution, February 6, 2018. https://www.brookings.edu/blog/order-from-chaos/2018/02/06/trumps-nuclear-plan-mostly-makes-sense.

Oppenheimer, J. Robert. *The Open Mind*. New York: Simon & Schuster, 1955.

Petrucelli, Joe. “Assessing Denuclearization in the Post-Cold War Era.” *RealClearDefense*, September 20, 2017. https://www.realcleardefense.com/articles/2017/09/20/assessing_denuclearization_in_the_post-cold_war_era_112340.html.

“Post-Cold War World.” Atomic Heritage Foundation, June 19, 2014. https://www.atomicheritage.org/history/post-cold-war-world.

Putin, Vladimir. “Presidential Address to the Federal Assembly.” President of Russia, March 1, 2018. http://en.kremlin.ru/events/president/news/56957.

Riminton, Hugh, Richard Roth, Barbara Starr, and Susie Xu. “U.N. Slaps Trade, Travel Sanctions on North Korea.” CNN, October 15, 2006. http://www.cnn.com/2006/WORLD/asiapcf/10/14/nkorea.sanctions/index.html.

Sampathkumar, Mythili. "US-North Korea Summit: A Timeline of the Tumultuous Relations between the Two Nations." *Independent* (UK), May 24, 2018. https://www.independent.co.uk/news/world/asia/trump-us-north-korea-summit-kim-jong-un-timeline-history-relationship-a8367651.html.

Shanker, Tom. "U.S. Says Iran Has Material for an Atomic Bomb." *New York Times*, March 1, 2009. http://www.nytimes.com/2009/03/02/washington/02military.html?_r=2&hp.

Tannenwald, Nina. "Justice and Fairness in the Nuclear Nonproliferation Regime." *Ethics & International Affairs* 27, no. 3 (2013): 299–317. https://pdfs.semanticscholar.org/9d47/cdb6b49d875711b3e00298fb504aa72e82ff.pdf

"Timeline of Events: Iran Nuclear Deal 2009 Onwards." *TRT World*, May 8, 2018. https://www.trtworld.com/americas/timeline-of-events-iran-nuclear-deal-2009-onwards-17299.

Younger, Stephen M. *Endangered Species: How We Can Avoid Mass Destruction and Build a Lasting Peace*. New York: HarperCollins, 2007.

INDEX

Page numbers in **boldface** are illustrations.

ABOUT THE AUTHOR

Erin L. McCoy is a literature, language, and cultural studies educator and an award-winning photojournalist and poet. She holds a master of arts degree in Hispanic studies and a master of fine arts in creative writing from the University of Washington. She has edited nearly twenty nonfiction books for young adults, including *The Mexican-American War* and *The Israel-Palestine Border Conflict* from the Redrawing the Map series with Cavendish Square Publishing. She is from Louisville, Kentucky.